Love,
Faith and Forgiveness

Love,
Faith and Forgiveness

Ai Snell

XULON PRESS

Xulon Press
2301 Lucien Way #415
Maitland, FL 32751
407.339.4217
www.xulonpress.com

Paperback ISBN-13: 978-1-66288-236-4
Hard Cover ISBN-13: 978-1-66288-237-1
Ebook ISBN-13: 978-1-66288-238-8

TABLE OF CONTENTS

A Devotional Study Guide is given at the end of the
book that is designed to encourage you to receive God's
love on a daily basis as you journey through your own
walk of faith. Read my story and then use the days indi-
cated to do a more in-depth study of the scriptures and
concepts presented in each chapter.

INTRODUCTION

I am the way, the truth, and the life. No one comes unto the Father except through Me.
(Jesus in John 14:6)

I just want to introduce myself. Like all of us, I was created by God (see Genesis 1:27). God gave us life. He gave each of us a piece of His heart and that is enough to sustain us, though we live in challenging times.

Many people fear the future, worrying about how to earn a living, will they find love, and how can they become successful. In contrast to this, God gives us His love and asks us to love Him in return (see Day 1. Matthew 6:25-34).

God asks us to accept the gift of His one and only begotten Son, Jesus. As we travel this road of life, He fills the way with hope and provides us with the material things and power we need to move forward to an increasingly better life as we turn to

Him as our source (see Day 2. Hebrews 12:1-3 and Philippians 4:19).

God wants us to strengthen our spiritual life with His everlasting love that will overcome the hate and chaos of this world. His Word tells us it is faith, hope, and love that provides the foundation for our daily lives (see Day 2. 1 Corinthians 13:13).

Like rivers of grace, His love flows into each of our lives assuring us of His forgiveness and that this life is only temporary. Knowing this, we must not judge one another. None of us is perfect. God uses our contact with each other to help shape us into the people He has intended us to be.

Faith without love is cold and unfeeling. Hope without love is worthless. Unforgiveness is a sin, but love is the fire that ignites our faith and produces the light of hope that affirms His presence in our lives.

My prayer is that as you read about my ups and downs and walk out your journey of faith, you will experience God's love every step of the way.

Pause for a Moment and Reflect…

> *As you read through my journey, consider the grace our Heavenly Father has bestowed on you. Take a moment to stop and read Luke 23:34.*

What did Jesus ask the Father to do for us?

Why did Jesus ask that of His Father?

My Lord, we share Your thirst for peace among Your people and Your hunger for Your love to manifest in our lives. Rouse us to desire to drink from Your living water. May we embrace the amazing sacrifice of Your Son on the cross and take to heart the loving words He spoke while He willingly gave His lifeblood for our salvation and forgiveness.

Read the last words of Jesus before He died:

John 19:26-28
Luke 23:43
Mark 15:34
John 19:30
Luke 23:46

Dear Lord, all these words You spoke before You died were meant to wake up our souls. May we pray daily for You to give us our daily bread and forgive us our trespasses as we forgive those who trespass against us. Lead us not into temptation but deliver us

> *from evil. Jesus, please fill our hearts with a deep longing for You, today and every day. Thank You that at Your empty tomb we can find true life, forgiveness, and hope. Thank You, Jesus, that through Your great love, we can draw close to the Father and experience the power and guidance of Your Holy Spirit. Amen*

Go to Days 1 and 2 in the devotional study guide at the end of this book for a more in-depth study of the scriptures and concepts shared in this introduction.

CHAPTER 1
GOD IS LOVE

For God so loved the world that He gave His one and only Son, that whoever believes in Him should not perish but have eternal life. (John 3:16)

I am so thankful to my Heavenly Father that I have a new heart and a new spirit within me. I thank the Father that He has taken my stony heart out and replaced it with a heart filled to the brim with love. I can love my friends, my family, I can even love my enemies because of what God has done for me and in me. God has truly replaced my heart of stone with a heart of flesh. He has given me a new heart and placed a new spirit within me that reflects His love and His purpose. I am thankful I can love God with all my heart, with all my soul, and all my strength (see Day 3).

Jesus told His disciples that there were two great commandments. "You shall love the Lord your God with all your heart, with all your soul, and with all your mind.' This is the first and great commandment. And the second is like it. 'You shall love your neighbor as yourself.' On these two commandments hang all the Law and the Prophets" (Matthew 22:37-40).

God has revealed to me that He has also given me a wonderful mind and He has a plan and purpose for my life here on the earth (see Day 3: Mark 16:15-16). Part of my assignment is to help my Buddhist family to come to know of His great love. I was raised Buddhist. My father was a musical person and my mother was a housewife. I came from a big family. I have two brothers and three sisters. I love my family very much. We grew up together in what we believed was a wonderful life. A time came, however, when my father had to work far away from home. I was six years old at the time and stayed with my mom in the small village at Luang Prabng in Vientiane Laos. My father came back and decided he wanted to move our whole family to South Vietnam. I grew up and was educated there. I was sent to a Catholic school and learned French for nine years.

Pause for a Moment and Reflect...

Read Ezekiel 11:19-20.

What is the promise from God in these verses?

Read Jeremiah 29:11-13.

What are His promises in these verses?

When I turned thirteen, the Communists came in and took over the South. My family fell apart. My mother moved to America with my older sister, who had been educated in the US and had chosen to stay there. The American Embassy would only allow three members of our family to relocate to the United States at a time. Therefore, my brother, my other sister, and I stayed with my father until we could make arrangements to join my mother and sister in America.

The delay caused us to be stuck there with the Communists in control. We lived in sadness day to day without my mother. At thirteen, I really missed my mother's influence. I was growing into a young woman and began to feel empty, with no hope for the future. I didn't know how to deal with life anymore.

My father was lonely and depressed and developed a friendship with another woman. Though I was happy for my father that he had another friendship with this woman, it made it even more difficult for me. My brother and sister got jobs and moved out. I kept trying to forget about the past. In order to survive, I needed to live one day at a time. Then this other woman became my stepmother. I tried to adjust to this new life for my father's sake, but my stepmother was not happy with my presence in her new household. I often heard her and my father arguing over my presence there with them. Finally, she told me that I had to go out and look for a job.

To keep the peace, I left home at the age of fifteen. On my first night on my own, I slept in the graveyard maintenance building. I thank God for watching over and protecting me that night. I learned an important truth about God that night all alone out in the world.

"When my father and my mother forsake me, then the Lord will take care of me" (Psalm 27:10 see Day 4)

When I woke the next morning, I had nowhere to go. I decided to ask a friend from the Catholic school if I could stay with her family for a couple of days until I knew what to do with myself. She seemed to have the perfect life. It was the life I had always dreamed of. I longed to have someone to share my life with, love me, and we would make a wonderful family like my friend. I wished for a good man to spend the rest of my life with.

Finally, I found a French family looking for someone young and strong to take care of a sick elderly family member. I was happy to accept this work. Every day, I poured out my love and care to bring happiness to this sick person. I believed this was what I was called to do with my life. I believed God had given me this gift of love to share and to do whatever I was doing with love. I thanked God every day for continually filling me with His love.

In Matthew 10:42, Jesus told His disciples, "And whoever gives one of these little ones only a cup of cold water in the name of a disciple, assuredly I say to you, he shall by no means lose his reward" (see Day 5).

My Dream

One night, I dreamed a gentle man came to me with a beautiful heart. I dreamed he was holding my hand and we were walking together in the rain. When he looked into my eyes, I knew I could give my heart to him and he would take care of me.

My life was very hard at this point, but I accepted that this was where God wanted me to be, helping these people. I knew that He had equipped me to overcome every obstacle in this world. He led me through all my losses and used this opportunity to teach me how to truly love others. The road I was traveling was to teach me to be there for others who felt hopeless and were filled with sickness. I found I could not walk away from someone who needed my help. I thanked God that I was being filled with the knowledge of His will for me in all wisdom and spiritual understanding. I thanked Him that I was constantly learning His ways and purposes (see Day 5).

I found as I followed this path that He was also giving me spiritual discernment. My constant prayer was that I would walk worthy of His calling and be fruitful in doing good work, steadily growing and increasing in my knowledge of Him. I prayed that all my decisions were ordered by Him. Through everything I experienced, He reassured me that I was His beloved child and never alone. He was with me and His Holy Spirit showed me that I would share in the inheritance of being His child and a joint heir with Jesus.

Pause for a Moment and Reflect...

Read 2 Peter 1:3-4 (also see Day 6).

What assurance did you receive from these verses?

*What has God given you to help you escape
the corruption of the world around you?*

As I diligently worked to fulfill His purpose for my life, He showed me clearly that I was His temple and His Spirit dwelled within me, giving me the power to overcome whatever I faced in life with His love and compassion for others. Each time I was called to go through something painful, He showed me to claim His promises. When I was hungry, He gave me food. When I was thirsty, He provided drink. When I was cold, He sent His warmth and when I was lonely, He came to visit me.

As I worked and cared for others, God continually pressed upon me that no matter whether we are rich or poor, we all have the same destination. We all need God to guide us through our individual journeys (see Day 6).

Pause for a Moment and Reflect…

As you read how God had begun to guide me through my journey, consider the great love your Heavenly Father has bestowed on you. What He has done for me He will surely do for you.

Read John 3:16.

What is the precious promise God has given you in this verse?

Read Galatians 6:10.

What does this verse encourage each of us to do?

Dear Lord, I thank You that You guide us along our journey as we seek to fulfill Your plan and purpose in our lives. Continually fill us with Your love so we can pour that love out on others we encounter on our life's journey. Thank You for meeting our needs along our journey and that we can claim Your promises in our lives as we move forward to our ultimate destination.

Thank You, Father, for Your Son who gave His life to bring me life. I pray I will walk worthy of Your great love.

Go to Days 3 through 6 in the devotional study guide at the end of this book for a more in-depth study of the scriptures and concepts shared in this chapter.

Ai Snell Age Sixteen

CHAPTER 2
The Phone Call

"The Spirit of the Lord God is upon Me, Because the Lord has anointed Me to preach good tidings to the poor; He has sent Me to heal the brokenhearted, To proclaim liberty to the captives, and the opening of the prison to those who are bound; To proclaim the acceptable year of the Lord, and the day of vengeance of our God; to comfort all that mourn." (Isaiah 61:1-2)

One day, as I was spending time alone with the Lord, I received a phone call. When I picked up the phone to answer it, I wondered who would call this early in the morning. A man with a gentle voice began to talk to me. I was thinking he must have the wrong number, so I hung up. I never expected him to call back, but he called again the next morning. I answered the phone and he introduced himself. He sounded very nice. We had a very pleasant conversation. I felt comfortable talking with him and felt he was a friendly, gentle person. I was lonely and felt he could be my friend.

The week passed, and as we talked almost daily, we started to understand more and more about one another. I enjoyed our conversations and a friendship began to grow between us. These phone conversations continued over the next three months. Because of our work obligations, we didn't have time to meet one another face-to-face. As our lives became even busier, I found I missed hearing his voice if we could not talk on the phone.

By this time, I thought to myself, "God has given me this man." Our friendship grew and now we talked every night on the phone. Though we still had not met in person, he began to send me flowers every week. Then he sent me a picture of himself and I felt so happy. I believed he was the man from my dream. I thanked God that He loved me so much, He brought this man into my life.

As our phone calls continued, I felt I knew him and began to share my hopes and desires for the future with him. Our calls every night brought such joy into my life. I knew I was growing to love him and did not want to live life without him. We then made a commitment to one another to continue our relationship until we could be together. I began to picture myself as a good wife to him. I had so many good thoughts about him, my love for him, and our future together. I wanted to know all about his life, to share his love, and understand all he had been through. As he shared his life with me, I felt we were so perfect for each other. I wanted to convey to him how much I wanted to be there for him no matter what conditions we might face.

After six months of talking on the phone, I wanted to set up a time to meet him. The day we were going to meet, he called and want to change it at the last minute. The next night he called me later than normal and didn't sound like himself. He did not talk much and when he did say something, he sounded like he was depressed. I kept asking him if anything was wrong. Finally, he told me that he loved me and could not keep things hidden from me any longer. He apologized and said the man in the pictures he had been sending me was not him. It was just the picture of a man he had found in a magazine.

After the shock of hearing him admit that he had deceived me, I did not know what to do. I felt like I just wanted to run away. I could not handle what was happening in my life. I told him I needed to hang up and be alone for a few days.

For the next three days, I spent time with God and tried to get back to reality. The man of my dreams had disrespected me. I asked God to heal my pain, help me to forgive him, forget him, and to give me direction for my life.

The man tried to call me again and said he wanted to talk to me and tell me how over the last six months talking to me on the phone, he realized he had fallen in love with me. However, everything he had told me about his life was not true. I felt I could not love this man who had so deceived me, so I refused to talk to him.

For the next three weeks, he continued to try and reach me. He even said before he talked to me on the phone, he had no life. I wondered if I even wanted to continue any kind of friendship with such a man or should I just walk away completely. I could not decide, so I chose to take some time off and go away by myself. I continued to pray and ask God to help him find the life he needed, but at the same time, I didn't know what God would have me to do with all the beautiful dreams and memories of our conversations together. As I prayed and asked God to heal my pain and restore my life, I felt Him beginning to put my heart back together again.

Pause for a Moment and Reflect...

> *"The Spirit of the Lord God is upon Me,*
> *Because the Lord has anointed Me to preach*

good tidings to the poor; He has sent Me to heal the brokenhearted, To proclaim liberty to the captives, and the opening of the prison to those who are bound; To proclaim the acceptable year of the Lord, and the day of vengeance of our God; to comfort all that mourn." (Isaiah 61:1-2)

Father, even though my heart has been broken, I thank You that You did not leave me to try and gather all the pieces and attempt to put my heart back together again by myself. I thank You for sending Jesus to fulfill Isaiah 61:1 and healing my broken heart. I thank You that Your love is putting my heart back together again and making it whole. I thank You that I can cast all my cares upon You for You care for me.

Go to Days 7 and 8 in the devotional study guide at the end of this book for a more in-depth study of the scriptures and concepts shared in this chapter.

CHAPTER 3

A HEALING IN MOSCOW

For in Him we live and move and have our being." (Acts 17:28)

As I prayed and asked God to continue the healing of my heart, He led me to take a trip to the beautiful city of Moscow. By this time, I was older and able to change jobs. I was working as a hotel front desk clerk and was allowed to travel alone. The weather was lovely in Moscow and I began to recover from the shock and trauma of the man's betrayal and deception. This beautiful place gave me time to think and to focus on God's plans for my life. God began to show me that I was not in control of my life, He was. Only through surrendering to His plan and purpose could I truly be happy.

Pause for a Moment and Reflect...

Explain what Acts 17:28 means as we deal with the issues we face in our journey of life:

_____

_____

_____

What do we need to do to be truly happy no matter what we are facing along the way?

_____

_____

_____

What does surrendering to God's plan and purpose mean to you at this point in your own journey?

_____

_____

_____

I spent a week in Moscow and was overjoyed to find so many churches there. I thoroughly enjoyed visiting one after another. The last church I visited before I headed home was the Moscow Cathedral of Immaculate Conception. I had decided to spend my last evening in this beautiful church. As I entered the church, a man walked up behind me. He told me the mass would not start for another hour. I told him I just wanted to sit and pray if that was alright. He said I could stay and I sat off in the corner alone and quietly prayed by myself waiting for the mass.

My Vision

I must have fallen asleep or passed out.

In my vision/dream, I heard the bell go off signaling the beginning of the mass. I walked out of the church in time to see the most beautiful sunset I had ever seen. I thanked God for blessing me with such beauty. As my dream continued, God showed me a vision of my future life:

I realized the man who had told me the mass would not start for another hour had followed me out of the church.

He said, "You look like you are new to this city."

I was too nervous to respond, but I smiled at him, nonetheless.

When he smiled back at me, I suddenly felt such joy. It was as if God had sent this man to show me just how much He wanted my heart to heal.

The man asked me if he could walk with me and introduce me to his beautiful city. He said he had grown up here and loved to share it with visitors. We walked together around the corner and he invited me to have a hot chocolate with him at a little café. We walked some more and enjoyed the beautiful evening together. It was getting late, so he offered to drive me back to my hotel. I agreed as I did not want to try to find my way back in the dark. When I returned to my hotel and prepared to fly out the next morning, I realized God had healed my heart and filled me with hope once again.

As my dream/vision continued, I returned home and went back to my job at the hotel. Then I received a call from the man I had met in Moscow. He declared he had enjoyed our time together and wanted to continue our relationship, though he had to remain in Moscow and complete his four years at the Harvard School of Engineering and Applied Sciences. He vowed we would continue to talk on the phone every night until we could be together again.

I was nineteen and he was twenty-six. As our relationship continued, the love between us grew. We became committed to one another. He realized that it was very important that he be completely honest with me. He shared about his life quite openly. He had two children from his previous marriage. His son was six years old and his daughter was four. He asked me if I was comfortable knowing about that part of his life.

I responded, "I am yours. I love you. I am looking to build a life with you. Your past does not have to affect our future. I am here for you. I would like to meet your children and learn to love them as well."

I loved him very much. He was always there for me and gave me hope. I promised him my life and told him I would make him a good wife and a good mother for his children.

As my dream/vision continued, he completed his four years of school and we planned to meet again. He came to see me three weeks after his graduation and spent a couple of months with me getting to know me. The more time we spent together, the more I knew he was the man I had dreamed of all my life. I told him God gave me his heart and I would stay with him for the rest of my life.

We planned our wedding and decided to honeymoon in Paris for one week. Then my husband went to work each day and I stayed at home to care for the children and our home. On my birthday, I planned a surprise for my husband. I told him I was two months pregnant with our child. He was so happy! He told me I had brought such joy into his life. He worked hard every day to provide for our family and nourished our relationship. My job was to take care of my husband and our children and prepare for the birth of our new baby.

As I happily watched the vision continue, our family life settled into a routine and our children grew. I told my husband I desired for our children to attend Catholic school as I did. His children brought so much joy into my life. I quickly grew to love them very much. Then God gave us a newborn son as a special gift for my husband and me. We thanked God for giving us such wonderful gifts in our children, our love for one another, and the prosperity He brought into our lives.

Pause for a Moment and Reflect...

I encourage you to thank God daily for His presence and love in your life.

> *Father God, I have so many reasons to rejoice in You. I rejoice in Your presence in my life and for each new day that You have given me to live, to love, to enjoy, and to help others. I rejoice that I am Your child and that You love me and my family more than we love ourselves. I thank You for the*

gift of Your Son to show me the way of forgiveness.

God blessed me with a wonderful husband and his two beautiful children. I thanked God for the special gift He gave us with the addition of our new-born son. I gave all my children back to God and asked Him to guide us in raising them to become godly, productive adults. We knew we needed God in our lives and continually sought His direction for our lives.

Go to Days 9-11 in the devotional study guide at the end of this book for a more in-depth study of the scriptures and concepts shared in this chapter.

CHAPTER 4
GROWING TOGETHER IN THE LORD

"But seek first the kingdom of God and His righteousness, and all these things shall be added to you." (Matthew 6:33)

Time went by in my dream/vision and we had many wonderful times together as a family. Our faith in God helped us raise our children to seek Him first in their decisions in life. We prayed together as a family for one another. I prayed every day for my children and my husband that our Heavenly Father would give them strength when they were feeling weak and wisdom to guide them through their daily lives. We taught them to rejoice in the blessings of family, health, and friends and that these blessings were from God. We also taught them that in times of need, Jesus said they could come to Him and He would give them rest. They knew of God's great love from them and truly sought His plan for their lives.

> *And my God shall supply all your need according to His riches in glory by Christ Jesus.* (Philippians 4:19)

I am so proud of my kids. Our sons wanted to go to the University in northern Italy to study Theology. I was so happy they wanted to become priests and serve the Lord. Our daughter wanted to study nursing and serve the Lord helping others in that way. I thanked God every day for His love and what He had done in our family.

Then my dream took a serious, painful turn. One night, my husband took me in his arms, held me tight, looked into my eyes, and said, "I love you very much. I want to stay with you forever, but something has happened that I must tell you about."

"What has happened?" I asked him.

"I have not told you this before because I did not want to worry you until I had a better idea of what was going on with my health. For the last month, I have been in a great deal of pain. After a series of tests, the doctor has diagnosed me with kidney failure. The test they performed showed that I have kidney cancer."

I was totally shocked and cried most of the night as my beloved husband held me in his arms and tried to comfort me. We prayed together and asked God for wisdom as to what to do next.

The next day, I took my husband to see the doctor. The doctor told us the only option at this point was to have a kidney transplant. He warned us that there was no guarantee we could even get on the list, but we quickly accepted this option and asked him to proceed. I told the doctor I wanted to see if I could give my husband one of mine. I was willing to do whatever I could to help my husband live.

After many blood tests, we were in the hospital to share the gift of life with each other. God gave me life to share with my husband and I was able to give him a kidney.

After we came home, I was determined to spend every second of my life with my beloved husband. I loved him so much and knew a big part of my job now was to be an encouragement to my husband. I reminded him that even though our children were grown now, we all still needed him to stay positive. Our oldest son was now twenty-six years old, our daughter was twenty-four, and Alyosha was nineteen. My husband was too weak to work, so I applied for and God blessed me with a job at the hospital.

After our youngest son graduated from high school, he decided to postpone going away to university to spend time with his father and to help care for him. The two of them were very close. He told his father that he wanted to follow in his footsteps and go to engineering school. He was so glad he chose to spend that special time with his father as his condition worsened very rapidly.

Day-by-day, I spent as much time as possible with my beloved husband. Our oldest son went away to college and our daughter now worked with the Red Cross far away from home. Her work sent her to West Africa to do missions work there for three months.

My dream/vision now moved to the anniversary of our marriage. My husband said he wanted to go to Russia to visit where he came from and to celebrate our upcoming anniversary there. We wanted to visit where we met and visit his hometown of Saint Petersburg. My husband suggested we have a re-marriage ceremony at the Cathedral Immaculate Church where we were first married. We had so many wonderful memories of our original time in Moscow. We thanked God for bringing us together.

After our amazing anniversary trip, we flew back home. Our first night home, my husband took me in his arms and talked to me about his love for me. He thanked me for letting him into my life. He told me how much he loved me and held me tight.

Suddenly, he said he was very tired and passed out. I stayed next to him, listening for his heartbeat. I told him I loved him very much. At 3:00 a.m. on Friday morning, he took his last breath...

Pause for a Moment and Reflect...

Pause and thank God today for the wonderful blessings He has given you.

> *Thank You, Father God, for Your goodness is overwhelming. Thank You for giving so bountifully in my life and for this beautiful family You have given me. Thank You for Your Son who so willingly gave His life for me.*

Go to Days 12-13 in the devotional study guide at the end of this book for a more in-depth study of the scriptures and concepts shared in this chapter.

CHAPTER 5
MY DREAM COMES TRUE

Suddenly, I heard the bell go off signaling the beginning of the mass. When I opened my eyes, there was nobody around me. I was all by myself sitting in the corner of the church in Moscow. Realizing I had been dreaming, I stood up and walked out of the church. My eyes were still wet after experiencing such a vivid vision from God. As I stood outside the church looking up at the cross and praying, I was suddenly aware there was a man standing there praying at the cross not far from me.

As he turned around and looked at me, he said with his eyes, "You are the woman I have been searching for in my mind for a very long time."

He walked over to me with a smile on his face and introduced himself, "I'm Alexander. It's cold out here. I can give you a ride home and if you are hungry, we can stop by a restaurant and eat something."

We did go and get something to eat and talked for most of the evening. I almost immediately trusted Alexander.

Alexander told me, "I have been coming and standing and praying at the cross outside the church for almost two years. I have felt like I was missing something. Today when I arrived, it was like the Lord said, this is the day to receive."

Then he prayed, "Father, Your goodness is overwhelming. My joy is filled to running over. Thank You, Father, that Jesus told us that whatever we ask in His name, You will give to us. I rejoice and give thanks that the name of Jesus has such power and authority. I'm blessed to ask in the name of Jesus because of the love that filled my heart is the sweet expectation of receiving what I ask for from You. Thank You for giving so bountifully in my life this beautiful woman that my joy is running over."

From that day forward, my life changed forever. First of all, I realized I had forgiven the man from the phone relationship. I was young and lonely and had experienced "puppy love," but that was all it was. Now, I was about to start the life God had ordained for me. The vision/dream He had revealed to me in the church was about to come true. I thanked God for healing my heart and giving me new hope for the life ahead of me.

For the next year, Alexander and I started getting to know each other. Alexander came to see me and we spent a lot of time together. I was working as a hotel front desk clerk and he stayed at the hotel where I worked. He said he had a long vacation and wanted to use it to get to know me better. He stayed for three months and then went back home.

The next time he came to visit me, we became engaged and began to plan our wedding. Unlike my dream, Alexander had not been married before and did not have any children prior to our marriage. We decided since most of his family lived in Russia, we would be married in the church where we met. Then we stayed there and lived in Russia to raise our family.

Unlike my dream, we had four children together, three boys and one girl. Their names are Alyoshenka, Alyosha, Elena, and Afonka.

From then on, my life happened just like it did in my dream. All our kids grew up and went to Catholic school. Both of our older sons went to Italy to go to college in Rome and studied theology to prepare to become priests. Our only daughter, Elena, went through the nursing program and then joined the Red Cross. Our youngest son, Afonka, looked the most like his father and was very close with his father. He always told my husband he wanted to be a technical engineer like Alexander.

After my husband was diagnosed with cancer, Afonka delayed going to college to spend the time with his father and help with his care. I was very grateful for his help and support.

Looking back, I suspect my husband had been ill for quite a while, but he did not tell me he was in so much pain. He wanted to continue providing for us and did not want me to worry. When it became obvious he was tired all the time, I insisted we go to the doctor. Just like in my dream, his prognosis was not good and I offered to give him one of my kidneys to prolong his life. He was the most important man in my life and I would do anything to help him. I had learned how to care for the sick back when I was only fourteen and working for the French family. Now, I would take care of my beloved husband.

We had shared our lives together for nearly twenty-seven years. My husband was fifty-three and I was forty-six when he became so very ill.

We did indeed go back to Moscow to the church where we were married to celebrate our anniversary and renew our marriage vows. When we came back home, my beloved husband did die in my arms on Friday, at 3.a.m. That is a day I will never forget! I felt lost and empty in my heart, but God gave me the strength to handle all of my responsibilities.

After my husband passed away, my son, Afonka was so sad. He would not talk much. Each time I looked at my son, it brought back memories of my husband. He looks so much like his father, it made me feel lonely and so sad at our loss.

During this time, I worked to help my son decide to finish his schooling. He decided he wanted to move up north to Rome to study up there with his brothers.

> *My God, I have done my job to care for my children and my husband. Even as I promised You when each of my children was born, I have given them all to You, to serve You, and to follow Your Words. Please guide them. My heart, soul, and spirit belong to You. Thank You, Father, for showing us that You love us so much. There is no excuse for us not loving one another. Thank You, Lord, for giving me a soft heart and the ability to love my brothers and sisters on this earth. I know I could never do this on my own, but because You love me through all my sin, all my faults, and all my failures, You give me the ability to love even those people who seem unlovable and forgive those who have hurt me.*

> *Thank You, Father, for Your Word that teaches us that everyone deserves love and forgiveness.*

My husband had told me he wanted to be buried back home in the cemetery in the tombs of Alexander Nevsky in St. Petersburg, Russia. So, I had to move up there to be near him. That was to be my home now. By this time, I was feeling very lonely in my heart and soul. I missed my husband every day. He had always been there for me. Whenever I cried, he would come to me and give me a hug to show me how much he cared for me. When I was lonely, he would come to me with his warm heart.

My Lord, the earth will someday pass away, but I will stand on Your promise all the days of my life. It lifts my spirit up to know all the spiritual blessings in heavenly places are mine. I give You praise and adoration because You are the Father of our Lord, Jesus Christ. I rejoice that Jesus is with You in heaven and is preparing a place for me there. I am ready for that wonderful day when He will come to take me home to You, Father. I feel lonely here and I miss You and I miss my husband. All the memories that You gave us both is the place for me to stand until that day. Every day I am still on this earth, I have to wait for You, miss You, and love You.

I still go to Your house at the Cathedral and wait for the bell. You allowed me to meet my husband there. He took my hand and we walked in the snow before he took me home. Our love is still fresh in all the memories in my spirit. You came for him and took him back into Your heart to a place where there is no pain, no tears, and where we will live forever and ever with You, our Father.

> *My Lord, I cannot live without You. You mean so much to me. You gave Your Son for my sins. Now I know He is watching over me every day because He lives in me. I rejoice that Jesus is the way, the truth, and the life and no one comes to the Father except through Him. Thank You, Jesus. I look forward to our reunion in heaven.*

Although I was very sad and missed my husband, my heart thanked my loving heavenly Father for all the beautiful memories He gave us while we were together here on this earth.

> *Dear God, I did not expect my life to happen like the dream You gave me that day in the beautiful church in Moscow. Such a special gift You gave me in the wonderful man who became my husband. He lived his life for our marriage and to build a wonderful*

relationship with me. He gave me four beautiful children—Alyoshenka, Alyosha, Elena, and Afonka. I am so thankful, Father, I have so many reasons to rejoice in the life You have given me and the amazing memories we all had together with Alexander Prosviryakovich.

CONCLUSION
AMAZING MEMORIES

As I lay alone in my bed, I thought of so many wonderful memories God gave me with my beloved husband. I am so thankful we had that time to spend our anniversary in Moscow before God took him home to heaven.

In my mind's eye, I continue to see how I walked out of the church where we met, were married, and then re-married. I remember how I stood by the cross feeling very lonely and a man was standing there by the cross praying. I picture in my mind how he turned, looked at me, smiled, and his gentle eyes seemed to say, "This is the woman I've been searching for a very long time."

As I watched the scene play out in my mind, the man came up to me, smiled, and introduced himself, "I'm Alexander. It's cold out here. I can give you a ride home and if you are hungry, we can stop by a restaurant and eat something...."

I have so many wonderful reasons to rejoice in You, Father. I rejoice in Your presence in my life. I rejoice in each new day you give us to live, to love, to enjoy, and to help others. I rejoice that I am Your child and that You love us all more than we love ourselves. I rejoice in Your words, in Your power, and in Your glory that I see in the world all around me. I rejoice in the blessings You have showered upon me day after day. I thank You for the blessings of joy, of health, of prosperity, of family, and of friends. I rejoice in the work You have given me to do and in the quiet times when I can come to You and worship You in spirit and in truth. Thank You that I can come to You with all my pain and hopelessness and You give me rest as You did when my husband became so very sick. I now know that all that happened to help me recognize how much I need You in my life.

Without problems, we might never call upon Your name!

Dear God, You are the wonderful Father who created us. Though You created this whole universe, it is not bigger than Your love for us. You created this all for us, but that was not enough. You then sent Your beloved Son to die for our sins. Father God, I love You with all my heart. Even with Your last breath on the cross, You forgave us and gave Your blood to wash our sins away.

Thank You, Father, for giving me Alexander. Thank You for the years we had together after marrying in that beautiful Moscow Cathedral. Thank You for the beautiful family You gave us. I thank You that our oldest sons were able to go to the University in Rome and study Theology. I thank You that our daughter could go to nursing school and then work for the Red Cross. I thank You that our younger son, who looks so much like his father, chose to postpone his education to spend time with Alexander at home. I thank You for that beautiful time we had in Moscow together as we celebrated our twenty-seventh anniversary. You gave me such a special gift in my husband. I thank You for the beautiful relationship we shared and the wonderful memories of our life together.

Dear Brothers and Sisters, sometimes we experience things in life that we find hard to understand. We must remember we are human beings, we are not perfect, and we do not see the whole picture. We must not judge one another. One of the things I have learned is to forgive each other for our mistakes and give love to one another just as God has done for us. As we forgive, we also receive forgiveness. Just like I never expected love to come to me, just remember God has plans for each one of us.

God, our Father, is the Creator and has a plan and purpose for each of our lives. He sent His beloved Son, Jesus, to forgive us for our sins and to open the way to a relationship with Him. Jesus has promised us that we can come to Him with all our pain and with all our hopelessness and He will give us rest. God loves us so much and will guide us through this life until it is time for us to join Him in heaven.

Whenever we need Him, we can just call on His name and He will guide us through the challenges, temptations, hopelessness, pain, and weakness in our hearts. We may have even been tempted to blame God, but truly God has a plan for each of our lives. As you read in my story, you saw how I needed God's help throughout my husband's sickness and death. God was there with me and never left me. He will do the same for you.

We are to be grateful and thank God for each new day. Ask Him to show you how to bring glory to His name.

Go to Day 14 in the devotional study guide at the end of this book for a more in-depth study of the Scriptures and concepts shared in this conclusion.

DISCOVERING GOD IS LOVE

Receiving the Love of God Daily in Your Faith Walk

Daily Devotional

This Devotional Study Guide is designed to encourage you to receive God's love on a daily basis as you journey through your own walk of faith.

Introduction

Many people fear the future, worrying about how to earn a living, will they find love, and how can they become successful. In contrast to this, God gives us His love and asks us to love Him in return. We will begin this series of daily devotionals studying what Jesus said in Matthew 6:25-34 concerning worry.

Day 1: Do Not Worry

> *"Therefore I say to you, do not worry about your life, what you will eat or what you will drink; nor about your body, what you will put on. Is not life more than food and the body more than clothing? Look at the birds of the air, for they neither sow nor reap nor gather into barns; yet your heavenly Father feeds them. Are you not of more value than they?* (Matthew 6:25-26)

Jesus asks us some very interesting questions as He encourages us not to worry. If you were talking with Jesus about worry, how would you answer His questions?

Is not life more than food and the body more than clothing?

_____

Look at the birds of the air, for they neither sow nor reap nor gather into barns; yet your heavenly Father feeds them. Are you not of more value than they?

_____

Why do you think Jesus began this discussion on worry asking us these questions?

_____

Now read what Jesus said in verses 28-32a.

> *"So why do you worry about clothing? Consider the lilies of the field, how they grow: they neither toil nor spin; and yet I say to you that even Solomon in all his glory was not arrayed like one of these. Now if God so clothes the grass of the field, which today is, and tomorrow is thrown into the oven, will He not much more clothe you, O you of little faith? Therefore do not worry, saying, 'What shall we eat?' or 'What shall we drink?' or 'What shall we wear?' For after all these things the Gentiles seek."*

What does Jesus say we lack if we worry about food and clothing?

_____

Who does He compare us to if we worry about these things?

_____

Now consider the question Jesus asks in verse 27: "Which of you by worrying can add one cubit [unit of measure] to his stature [or to the span of his life]?"

How would you answer this very important question?

_____

Jesus then explained how we should live our lives instead of worrying about food and clothing in verses 32b-34.

> *"For your heavenly Father knows that you need all these things. But seek first the kingdom of God and His righteousness, and all these things shall be added to you. Therefore do not worry about tomorrow...."*

What is our remedy for worry?

_____

Pray this prayer: *Thank You, heavenly Father, that You know all my needs and as I seek You first, I know You have promised to supply everything I need for my life's journey. Remind me daily that I need do not need to worry, but put my trust in You. Amen.*

Day 2
Race of Faith

To successfully endure the race of life that is set before us, we need to understand how to ignite our faith that God does indeed know about and wants to provide everything we need along the way. Begin by reading Hebrews 12:1-3.

> *Therefore we also, since we are surrounded by so great a cloud of witnesses, let us lay aside every weight, and the sin which so easily ensnares us, and let us run with endurance the race that is set before us, looking unto Jesus, the author and finisher of our faith, who for the joy that was set before Him endured the cross, despising the shame, and has sat down at the right hand of the throne of God.*

Who is the example we need to focus on to develop our faith for this journey?

_____

As we travel this road of life, God fills the way with hope and provides us with the material things and power we need to move forward to an increasingly better life as we turn to Him as our source.

Read Philippians 4:19. "And my God shall supply all your need according to His riches in glory by Christ Jesus."

What does God mean when He says He will supply **all** your needs?

_____

Are there needs He cannot or will not supply?

_____

Explain your answer:

_____

God wants us to strengthen our spiritual life with His everlasting love so that we can overcome the hate and chaos of this world. His Word tells us it is faith, hope, and love that provides the foundation for our daily lives.

> Read 1 Corinthians 13:13. **"And now abide faith, hope, love, these three; but the greatest of these *is* love."**

Define faith:

_____

Define hope:

_____

Define love:

_____

Why is love the most important character trait necessary to overcome the chaos and hate especially in our world?

_____

Like rivers of grace, His love flows into each of our lives assuring us of His forgiveness and that this life is only temporary. Knowing this, we must not judge one another. None of us is perfect. Unforgiveness is a sin, but love is the fire that ignites our faith and produces the light of hope that affirms His presence in our lives.

In Matthew 6:12 Jesus told His disciples to pray and ask God to, "Forgive us our debts, As we forgive our debtors." Then in verses 14-15, Jesus tells us why we need to forgive.

> *"For if you **forgive** men their trespasses, your heavenly Father will also **forgive** you. But if you do not **forgive** men their trespasses, neither will your Father **forgive** your trespasses."*

Pray this prayer: *Thank You, Jesus, that at Your empty tomb I can find true life, forgiveness, and hope. Thank You, Jesus, that through Your great love, I can draw close to the Father and experience the power and guidance of Your Holy Spirit. Show me how to activate my faith, trust my heavenly Father to provide my needs, and forgive others as You have forgiven me. Amen*

Day 3
Love God

I thank the Father that He has taken my stony heart out and replaced it with a heart filled to the brim with love so I can truly love Him as Jesus taught us to do.

Read Matthew 22:37-40.

Write out what Jesus told His disciples the two greatest commandments were:

The first is:

_____

The second is:

_____

God revealed to me that He has a plan and purpose for my life here on the earth.

Read Mark 16:15-16.

And He said to them, "Go into all the world and preach the gospel to every creature. He who believes and is baptized will be saved; but he who does not believe will be condemned."

What is the assignment Jesus gave to each of us as His disciple?

_____

_____

Part of my assignment was to help my Buddhist family to come to know of His great love.

Do you have members of your family who do not know of God's great love for them?

_____

How will you explain this great love to them?

_____

One way is to use John 3:16 to help them understand this good news.

For God so loved the world that He gave His one and only Son, that whoever believes in Him should not perish but have eternal life.

Pray this prayer: *Thank You Father God that You loved me so much, You sent Your only Son to forgive me from my sins and give me eternal life with You. Show me how to express Your great love to those I love. Amen.*

Day 4
God's Protection

I thank God for watching over and protecting me. I learned an important truth about God that night all alone out in the world.

What was the important truth God revealed to me from Psalm 27:10?

_____

_____

Read the following verses and record what you learn about God from each one.

Proverbs 18:10 says the Lord is

_____

Psalm 61:3-4 says when my heart is overwhelmed

_____

_____

What promise from Psalm 91 ministered the most to you at this point in your journey?

_____

_____

Pray and thank God for His protection using Psalm 63:7:

_____

_____

_____

Day 5
Show God's Love

Every day, I poured out my love and care to bring happiness to a sick person. I believed this was what I was called to do with my life. I believed God had given me this gift of love to share and to do whatever I was doing with love. I thanked God every day for continually filling me with His love.

In Matthew 10:42, Jesus told His disciples, "And whoever gives one of these little ones only a cup of cold water in the name of a disciple, assuredly I say to you, he shall by no means lose his reward."

What talent or gift has God given you to demonstrate His love to others?

_____

_____

How are you using this gift?

_____

My life was very hard at this point, but I accepted that this was where God wanted me to be, helping these people. I knew that He had equipped me to overcome every obstacle in this world. God led me through all my losses and used this opportunity to teach me how to truly love others.

Read 2 Timothy 3:16-17.

> *All Scripture is given by inspiration of God, and is profitable for doctrine, for reproof, for correction, for instruction in righteousness, that the man of God may be complete, thoroughly equipped for every good work.*

Why is it so important that you spend time reading God's Word daily?

_____

_____

I was being filled with the knowledge of His will for me in all wisdom and spiritual understanding and constantly learning His ways and purposes.
Read Romans 12:2.

> *And do not be conformed to this world, but be transformed by the renewing of your mind, that you may prove what is that good and acceptable and perfect will of God.*

What do you need to do to prove what is the good and acceptable and perfect will of God for you?

_____

What do you need to do daily to obey these instructions?

_____

_____

What does Ephesians 5:17 say we are if we do not understand what the will of the Lord is for our lives?

_____

_____

Pray this prayer: *Thank You, Father God, that I am being filled with the knowledge of Your will for me in all wisdom and spiritual understanding. I thank You that I can constantly learn Your ways and purposes for my life as I obey the instructions in Your Word. Amen*

Day 6
Spiritual Discernment

I found as I followed this path He had given me, He was also giving me spiritual discernment. My constant prayer was that I would walk worthy of His calling and be fruitful in doing good work, steadily growing and increasing in my knowledge of Him. I prayed that all my decisions were ordered by Him.

Read Proverbs 2:2-6.

So that you incline your ear to wisdom, And apply your heart to understanding; Yes, if you cry out for discernment, And lift up your voice for understanding, If you seek her as silver, And search for her as for hidden treasures; Then you will understand the fear of the Lord, And find the knowledge of

God. For the Lord gives wisdom; From His mouth come knowledge and understanding.

What does this passage tell you to do to obtain spiritual discernment?

_____

_____

Through everything I experienced, God reassured me that I was His beloved child and never alone. He was with me and His Holy Spirit showed me that I would share in the inheritance of being His child and a joint heir with Jesus.

Read Romans 8:16-17.

How does God assure you that you are His child and a joint heir with Jesus?

_____

_____

As I diligently worked to fulfill His purpose for my life, He showed me clearly that I was His temple and His Spirit dwelled within me, giving me the power to overcome whatever I faced in life with His love and compassion for others.

Read 2 Peter 1:5-8 and list the steps you need to take to be fruitful in the knowledge of Jesus Christ.

1. _____

2. _____

3. _____

4. _____

5. _____

6. _____

7. _____

Pray this prayer: *I pray that all my decisions are ordered by You. Thank You for reassuring me that I am Your beloved child and never alone. Thank You, Father God, that each time I have been called to go through something painful, You have shown me to claim Your promises. Amen.*

As I worked and cared for others, God continually pressed upon me that no matter whether we are rich or poor, we all have the same destination. We all need God to guide us through our individual journeys.

Day 7
God's Loving Comfort

Read Isaiah 61:1-2.

> *"The Spirit of the Lord God is upon Me,*
> *Because the Lord has anointed Me to preach*
> *good tidings to the poor; He has sent Me*
> *to heal the brokenhearted, To proclaim*
> *liberty to the captives, and the opening of*
> *the prison to those who are bound; To pro-*
> *claim the acceptable year of the Lord, and*
> *the day of vengeance of our God; to comfort*
> *all that mourn."*

Have you experienced betrayal in a relationship
that has left you with a broken heart?

_____

What four things does Jesus say He came to
do for you?

_____

_____

_____

_____

Read Psalm 147:3.

He heals the brokenhearted

And binds up their wounds [sorrows].

Have you experienced sorrow in your life?

_____

What promise does your loving heavenly Father give you in this verse?

_____

_____

As I prayed and asked God to heal my pain and restore my life, I felt Him beginning to put my heart back together again.

Pray this prayer: *I thank You, my Lord, that You care so much for me that You will heal my broken heart and sorrows and comfort me as I humble myself before You and obey Your instructions.*

Day 8
Humble Yourselves

I could not decide what I needed to do. I chose to take some time off and go away by myself. I continued to pray, humble myself before the Lord, and ask God to help him find the life he needed. I didn't know what God would have me to do with all the beautiful dreams and memories of our conversations together.

Read 1 Peter 5:7.

> *Therefore humble yourselves under the mighty hand of God, that He may exalt you in due time, casting all your care upon Him, for He cares for you.*

What is the first thing His Word tell you to do in these verses?

_____

What does it mean to humble yourself before God?

_____

What does God say He will do if you obey His instructions?

_____

Then what does He tell you to do?

Why does God tell you to do this?

Read <u>Psalm 34:18</u> and <u>Psalm 51:17</u>.

> *The Lord is near to those who have a broken heart, And saves such as have a contrite spirit.*

> *The sacrifices of God are a broken spirit, A broken and a contrite heart— These, O God, You will not despise.*

A contrite heart is very important in our relationship with God.

Define a contrite heart:

Read <u>Isaiah 57:15</u>b.

> *To revive the spirit of the humble, And to revive the heart of the contrite ones.*

What do these verses say God will do if we are humble and have a contrite heart?

Pray this prayer: *Thank You, Father, that as I can cast my cares on You because You care for me. As I humble myself before You and spend time seeking Your guidance, please guide me along the path You have chosen for me.*

Day 9
Discerning God's Will

It was time for me to focus on God's plans for my life. God began to show me that I was not in control of my life, He was. Only through surrendering to His plan and purpose could I truly be happy.

Read Proverbs 3:5-6.

Trust in the Lord with all your heart, and lean not on your own understanding; in all your ways acknowledge Him, and He shall direct your paths.

What three things do these verses encourage you to do so that you can be sure you are on the path God has chosen for you?

_____

_____

How much does God want you to trust Him?

_____

How many of your ways does He want you to acknowledge Him?

_____

Read Romans 12:1-2.

> **Present your bodies a living sacrifice, holy, acceptable to God, which is your reasonable service. And do not be conformed to this world, but be transformed by the renewing of your mind, that you may prove what is that good and acceptable and perfect will of God.**

What three things do these verses say you need to do so you can discern God's will for your life?

_____

_____

_____

How will you begin to renew your mind so that you are not conforming to the world's ideas and ways?

_____

Where can you discover God's good, perfect, and perfect way to do things and make decisions in your life?

_____

Pray this prayer: *Thank You, God, that as I trust in You with all my heart, acknowledge You in all I do, and transform my mind to Your ways by reading and studying Your Word, that You will reveal Your will my life.*

Day 10

Now hope does not disappoint, because the love of God has been poured out in our hearts by the Holy Spirit who was given to us. (Romans 5:5)

I realized God had healed my heart and filled me with hope once again.

Why does hope in God not bring disappointment?

_____

Then God blessed me with a wonderful husband and his two beautiful children. I thanked God for the special gift He gave us with the addition of our newborn son.

Read Jeremiah 17:7-8.

> *Blessed is the man who trusts in the Lord, and whose hope is the Lord. For he shall be like a tree planted by the waters, which spreads out its roots by the river, and will not fear when heat comes; but its leaf will be green, and will not be anxious in the year of drought, nor will cease from yielding fruit.*

What are the blessings the Lord promises when we put our trust and hope in Him?

_____

_____

I gave all my children back to God and asked Him to guide Alexander and me in raising them to become godly, productive adults. We knew we needed God in our lives and continually sought His direction for our lives.

Read Psalm 78:6-7.

> *That the generation to come might know them [commandments of the Lord], the children who would be born, that they may arise and declare them to their children, that they may set their hope in God, and*

not forget the works of God, but keep His commandments.

What responsibility has God given parents concerning the training of their children?

_____

Why is this so important?

_____

Read <u>Proverbs 22:6</u>.

> *Train up a child in the way he should go,*
> *And when he is old he will not depart from it.*

What is the training manual we should use to train up our children in the way they should go?

_____

Read <u>Joel 2:28</u>.

> *[God's Spirit Poured Out] "And it shall come to pass afterward That I will pour out My Spirit on all flesh; Your sons and your daughters shall prophesy, Your old men shall dream dreams, Your young men shall see visions.*

What is God's promise if we raise up our children in the way they should go according to Joel 2:28?

_____

Pray this prayer: *For You are my hope, O Lord God; You are my trust from my youth (Psalm 71:5). I will hope in You continually, and will praise You yet more and more (Psalm 71:14).*

Day 11
Forgiveness

This part of my journey reflects God's heart as it concerns forgiving others as He has forgiven us. Read what the Bible tells us about the importance of forgiveness.

And forgive us our debts, as we forgive our debtors. And do not lead us into temptation, but deliver us from the evil one. For Yours is the kingdom and the power and the glory forever. Amen. For if you forgive men their trespasses, your heavenly Father will also forgive you. (Matthew 6:12-14)

Why did Jesus say it was so important that we forgive others?

_____

_____

Therefore, as the elect of God, holy and beloved, put on tender mercies, kindness, humility, meekness, longsuffering; bearing with one another, and forgiving one another, if anyone has a complaint against another; even as Christ forgave you, so you also must do. (Colossians 3:12-13)

How much did Christ forgive you?

_____

How much then must you forgive others?

_____

Read The Parable of the Unforgiving Servant:

Then Peter came to Him and said, "Lord, how often shall my brother sin against me, and I forgive him? Up to seven times?"

Jesus said to him, "I do not say to you, up to seven times, but up to seventy times seven. Therefore the kingdom of heaven is like a certain king who wanted to settle accounts with his servants. And when he had begun to settle accounts, one was brought to him who owed him ten thousand talents. But as he was not able to pay, his master commanded that he be sold, with his wife and children and all that he had, and that payment be made. The servant therefore fell down before him, saying, 'Master, have patience with me, and I will pay you all.' Then the master of that servant was moved with compassion, released him, and forgave him the debt. But that servant went out and found one of his fellow servants who owed him a hundred denarii; and he laid hands on him and took him by the throat, saying, 'Pay me what you owe!' So his fellow servant fell down at his feet and begged him, saying, 'Have patience with me, and I will pay you all.' And he would not, but went and threw him into prison till he should pay the debt. So when his fellow servants saw what had been done, they were very grieved, and came and told their master all that had been done. Then his master, after he had called him, said to *him, 'You wicked servant! I forgave you all that debt because you begged me. Should you not also have had compassion on your fellow servant, just as I had pity on you?' And his master was angry, and delivered him to the torturers until he should pay all that was due to him. So My heavenly Father also will do to you if each of you, from his heart, does not forgive his brother his trespasses."*

(Matthew 18:21-35)

What did the master call the unforgiving servant?

_____

What was his punishment for not forgiving his fellow servant?

_____

What did Jesus say our punishment would be if we were like this unforgiving servant?

_____

Did Jesus say that those who have betrayed or hurt us need to repent before we forgive them?

_____

Ask God to reveal to you if there are those in your life you need to forgive so He can truly bless your life. List the names God brings to your mind and then forgive them one by one.

_____

_____

_____

_____

_____

_____

_____

Pray this prayer: *Thank You Father God that You have forgiven me for my sins past, present, and future. Thank You that Your love has given me freedom from the punishment for my sin. Show me daily those I also need to forgive as You have forgiven me. Help me to reflect Your love and forgiveness to others whether they repent to me or not.*

Day 12
God Is Your Source

> *"But seek first the kingdom of God and His*
> *righteousness, and all these things shall be*
> *added to you."* (Matthew 6:33)

Time went by and we had many wonderful times together as a family. Our faith in God helped us raise our children to seek Him first in their decisions in life. We prayed together as a family for one another on a daily basis. God was faithful to meet our needs all along our journey.

Why is it important to seek God first in all that we do?

_____

What does it mean to seek His righteousness?

_____

What does God say He will do if we obey these instructions from Jesus?

_____

I prayed every day for my children and my husband that our Heavenly Father would give them strength when they were feeling weak and wisdom to guide them through their daily lives.

> *Rejoice always, pray without ceasing, in every-
> thing give thanks; for this is the will of God
> in Christ Jesus for you.* (1 Thessalonians
> 5:16-18 emphasis added)

What does this verse say is the will of God in
Christ Jesus for you and your family? Note the
words that are emphasized.

_____

_____

_____

> *Confess your trespasses to one another,
> and pray for one another, that you may be
> healed. The effective, fervent prayer of a
> righteous man avails much.* (James 5:16)

What instructions are you given in this verse?

_____

_____

What happens when you follow these
instructions?

_____

Do you have an effective, fervent prayer life?

_____

Why is it important that you work to have this kind of prayer life?

_____

We taught our children to not to live a life of worry, but instead to be thankful and rejoice in the blessings of family, health, and friends and that these blessings were from God.

> *Be anxious for nothing, but in everything by prayer and supplication, with thanksgiving, let your requests be made known to God; and the peace of God, which surpasses all understanding, will guard your hearts and minds through Christ Jesus.* (Philippians 4:6-7 emphasis added)

What four things does this passage say we are to do? Note the emphasized words.

_____

_____

_____

What is the reward for following these instructions?

> Pray this prayer: *I will praise You, O Lord, with my whole heart; I will tell of all Your marvelous works (Psalm 9:1). I will be anxious for nothing, but in everything by prayer and supplication, with thanksgiving, I will let my requests be made known to You. I thank You for the peace which surpasses all understanding that will guard my heart and mind through Christ Jesus as we diligently pray for one another.*

Day 13

> *And my God shall supply all your need according to His riches in glory by Christ Jesus.* (Philippians 4:19)

We also taught our children that in times of need, Jesus said they could come to Him and He would give them rest. They knew of God's great love from them and truly sought His plan for their lives.

Read these promises and instructions we shared with our children from God's Word to us as His beloved children:

> *Is anyone among you sick? Let him call for the elders of the church, and let them pray over him, anointing him with oil in the name of the Lord. And the prayer of faith will save the sick, and the Lord will raise him up. And if he has committed sins, he will be forgiven. Confess your trespasses to one another, and pray for one another, that you may be healed. The effective, fervent prayer of a righteous man avails much. Elijah was a man with a nature like ours, and he prayed earnestly that it would not rain; and it did not rain on the land for three years and six months. (James 5:14-17)*

What does this verse say saves the sick?

_____

How will the person be forgiven of his sins?

_____

> *Now may He who supplies seed to the sower, and bread for food, supply and multiply*

> *the seed you have sown and increase the
> fruits of your righteousness, while you are
> enriched in everything for all liberality,
> which causes thanksgiving through us to
> God.* (2 Corinthians 9:10-11)

Who provides what we need to prosper?

What should this prosperity cause us to do?

> *So Jesus answered and said to them,
> "Assuredly, I say to you, if you have faith
> and do not doubt, you will not only do what
> was done to the fig tree, but also if you say
> to this mountain, 'Be removed and be cast
> into the sea,' it will be done. And whatever
> things you ask in prayer, believing, you will
> receive."* (Matthew 21:21-23)

How must you pray to receive what you are
praying for?

Be kindly affectionate to one another with brotherly love, in honor giving preference to one another; not lagging in diligence, fervent in spirit, serving the Lord; rejoicing in hope, patient in tribulation, continuing steadfastly in prayer; distributing to the needs of the saints, given to hospitality. (Romans 12:10-13)

How are we to react to tribulation?

Be anxious for nothing, but in everything by prayer and supplication, with thanksgiving, let your requests be made known to God; and the peace of God, which surpasses all understanding, will guard your hearts and minds through Christ Jesus. (Philippians 4:6-7)

What are we supposed to do instead of worrying?

Pray this prayer: *I thank You, Father God, for the many promises You have given us in Your Word. I praise and thank You for teachings us these things so we can teach them to our children and our children's children.*

Day 14
Hope for Eternal Life

Though my beloved husband had passed from this life to the next, as a Christian, my grief was accompanied by hope for eternal life.

For God so loved the world that He gave His one and only Son, that whoever believes in Him should not perish but have eternal life. (John 3:16)

Read these verses that brought comfort to me during my time of grieving:

And I give them eternal life, and they shall never perish; neither shall anyone snatch them out of My hand. (John 10:28)

For the wages of sin is death, but the gift of God is eternal life in Christ Jesus our Lord. (Romans 6:23)

However, for this reason I obtained mercy, that in me first Jesus Christ might show all longsuffering, as a pattern to those who are going to believe on Him for everlasting life. (1 Timothy 1:16)

And this is the testimony: that God has given us eternal life, and this life is in His Son. He who has the Son has life; he who does not have the Son of God does not have life. These things I have written to you who believe in the name of the Son of God, that you may know that you have eternal life, and that you may continue to believe in the name of the Son of God. (1 John 5:11-13)

Pray this prayer: *Thank You Father God for the gift of eternal life through Your Son, Jesus. I thank You that I can know that my loved ones who accepted this amazing gift of love from You and have passed on to the next life, are with You. I thank You, that when I too pass to the next life, I will be with my loved ones and with You for eternity.*

Final Word

Dear Brothers and Sisters, sometimes we experience things in life that we find hard to understand. We must remember we are human beings and we do not see the whole picture. God our Father is the Creator and has a plan and purpose for each of our lives. He sent His beloved Son, Jesus, to forgive us for our sins and to open the way to a relationship with Him. Jesus has promised us that we can come to Him with all our pain and with all our hopelessness and He will give us rest as we walk through our life's journey. God loves us so much and will guide us through this life until it is time for us to join Him in heaven.

> *For I know the thoughts that I think toward you, says the Lord, thoughts of peace and not of evil, to give you a future and a hope.* (Jeremiah 29:11)

> *Come to Me, all you who labor and are heavy laden, and I will give you **rest**. Take My yoke upon you and learn from Me, for I am gentle and lowly in heart, and you will find rest for your souls.* (Matthew 11:28-29)

Therefore my heart is glad, and my glory rejoices; My flesh also will rest in hope. (Psalm 16:9)

Please take the time each day to thank and worship your Heavenly Father for all the blessings and love He has bestowed upon you. Use these verses to praise and worship Him.

But the hour is coming, and now is, when the true worshipers will worship the Father in spirit and truth; for the Father is seeking such to worship Him. God is Spirit, and those who worship Him must worship in spirit and truth. (John 4:23-24)

Give unto the Lord the glory due to His name; Worship the Lord in the beauty of holiness. (Psalm 29:2)

Oh, worship the Lord in the beauty of holiness! Tremble before Him, all the earth. (Psalm 96:9)

Pray this prayer as you conclude this devotional journal: *I have so many wonderful reasons to rejoice in You, Father. I rejoice in Your presence in my life.*

I rejoice in each new day you give me to live, to love, to enjoy, and to help others. I rejoice that I am Your child and that You love me more than I love myself. I rejoice in Your words, in Your power, and in Your glory that I see in the world all around me. I rejoice in the blessings You have showered upon me day after day. I thank You for the blessings of health, of prosperity, of family, and of friends. I rejoice in the work you have given me to do and in the quiet times when I can come to You and worship You in spirit and in truth. Thank You that I can come to You with all my pain and hopelessness and You give me rest. I love You, Lord.